A Ding Darling Sampler

The Editorial Cartoons of Jay N. Darling

A Ding Darling Sampler

The Editorial Cartoons of Jay N. Darling

Compiled and edited by
Christopher D. Koss

The Maecenas Press
2004

Library of Congress Control Number: 2004111264
ISBN: 0-944266-30-4

Published by
The Maecenas Press
Mt. Pleasant, South Carolina

Distributed by
Publications Order Department
The University of Iowa
2222 Old Highway 218 South
Iowa City, Iowa 52242-1602
Tel. (800) 235-2665

For more information please visit
the J. N. "Ding" Darling Foundation website.
www.dingdarling.org

Foreword

Experts estimate that Jay Norwood "Ding" Darling (1876–1962) drew 15,000 editorial cartoons chronicling the history, trends, thoughts, and politics of the United States for the half-century from 1912 to 1962. Ding was famous for these editorial cartoons, which appeared in approximately 150 major daily newspapers throughout the United States and earned him two Pulitzer Prizes.

From two magnificent archives of Darling's work, 200 of his most representative cartoons have been selected. They provide a painless inoculation of common sense, insights into history from those who lived it, and a better understanding of our lives today.

All these cartoons were drawn before the advent of television, and many appeared before radio. Because newspapers were the primary source of public information and commentary during the first half of the century, Ding became a household word, and his cartoons had an enormous impact on national public opinion.

In viewing Ding's cartoons, we absorb perspective on contemporary problems and issues, most of which we incorrectly assume are unique to our time.

Acknowledgments

Without Ding Darling's wisdom, keen powers of observation, and accomplished drawing skills, this book would not have been possible. Ding was also my grandfather, who taught that people of very modest abilities can accomplish any goal they want, as long as they are willing to work hard at it.

There is no friend more cherished by an author than a good editor. I have had the support of several outstanding editors, all of whom have contributed their time and energies to help produce the final draft: David Lendt, Ding Darling's biographer; Judith Caulfield, book designer and Ding Darling's great-niece; Art Penniman, George Raad, and Richard Whitaker, all good friends and thoughtful men.

Despite having superb material with which to work and despite the help of my many editors, I could not have completed *A Ding Darling Sampler* without the enduring patience and loving support of my dearest friend and wife, Andrea Godin Koss.

Contents

Human Nature

Ding had an unerring insight into human nature. As people read their daily newspapers, they were frequently rewarded with a flash of self-recognition that brought a chuckle and better understanding.

The News—Foreign and Domestic

When we become depressed by television news full of violence, mayhem, abuse, and corruption, it's interesting to note that Ding Darling had the same reaction to his morning newspaper in 1947.

Famous Afterthoughts in History

When Ding was not treating serious subjects such as the need to conserve our nation's natural resources, he could have just plain fun with the frailties of the human race and its institutions.

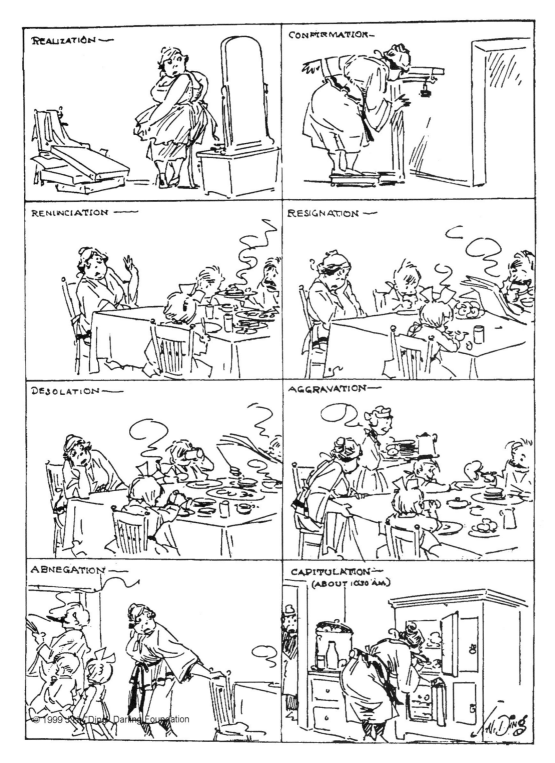

The Triumph of Matter over Mind

Few of Ding's readers knew that he wrote as well as he drew. His skilled use of words in this whimsical cartoon from 1932 gives a hint of how effective he was when writing on the conservation of the nation's natural resources.

Why Women Weep at June Weddings

When Ding was not dealing with such weighty subjects as war, peace and politics, he turned his attention to human nature. His delightful insights often sent his readers off to work with smiles on their faces.

Where Do Grandmothers Get All Their Old-Fashioned Ideas?

Grandmothers seem to have changed very little in the past half-century.

Recent Events Have Greatly Stimulated Interest in Aviation

Darling drew this cartoon following Lindbergh's successful crossing of the Atlantic in 1927. The event added to the challenge of mothering young boys and girls.

There Are Times When Nature Seems Particularly Unfair
in Her Distribution of Blessings

For a few days every summer we are particularly envious of youth.

Many Things Have Changed
in the Last Eight or Ten Million Years

There does seem to be less lust for knowledge these days.

10

Blaming It on the Bear

Ding drew this cartoon following the stock market crash of 1929. It seems to be human nature to blame something other than ourselves.

Virtue Is Its Own Reward

Cars today may look a bit different from this one that Darling drew in 1936,
but many drivers have harbored the same wishful thinking.

Had You Noticed How Much Shorter the Days Are Getting?

Even if you haven't been back to school in many a year,
you remember the feeling vividly.

THE ECLIPSE
IT'S DE DAY OF JUDGMENT
IT'S THE END OF THE WORLD
J. N. Ding
© 1999 J. N. "Ding" Darling Foundation

What a Lot of Difference a Little Knowledge of Astronomy Has Made in the Way We Feel Today

A little knowledge goes a long way.

Adventure in Discontent

Man's relationship with his automobile has not changed much this past century.

Never Again—Until the Next One Comes Along

Darling drew this cartoon following the great stock market crash of 1929. He observed in passing that "the public seems to need to be re-educated about every twenty years or so."

Add Postwar Readjustment Problems

Ding Darling was frequently credited with prescience. He always responded that it was easy to foresee the future if one paid any attention to the past. Nonetheless, he drew many cartoons for which there did not appear to be any precedent. Near the end of World War II, he forecast that the recently liberated female work force would not return eagerly to home and hearth.

Economics

Jay N. "Ding" Darling was an observant student of business and economics. Although most of us consider economic theory somewhat obscure and boring, Ding brought the subject to life with street-smart understanding.

BEFORE INFLATION - SHE GOES TO MARKET CARRYING HER MONEY IN HER **POCKET-BOOK** —

AND BRINGS HER GROCERIES HOME IN A **BASKET**.

AFTER INFLATION - SHE CARRIES HER **MONEY** IN A BASKET, AND BRINGS HER **GROCERIES** HOME IN HER POCKET-BOOK!

WORDS BY PHIL HANNA—MUSIC BY DING

The Housewife and Currency Inflation

Though inflation is tame as we enter the new millennium, most of today's shoppers recognize the same sinking feeling that Darling expressed in this 1940 cartoon.

The Class in Economics Will Please Come to Order

Even if students dress differently today, economic theory remains a fertile field for disagreement and faddish trends.

It's Fine As Long As You're Going Up

In March 1928, well before the stock market crash and panic of 1929, Ding began to draw a series of cartoons calling attention to the overvalued market.

How to Spank One of the Siamese Twins and Not Hurt the Other?

More than seventy years ago, the Federal Reserve Board began a series of interest rate increases in an attempt to curb stock market speculation. The challenge was to decrease investor enthusiasm without hurting business.

With his usual skill in reducing complex issues to basics, Darling conveyed the dilemma facing the Board in this cartoon published April 11, 1929.

Blowing Himself a Fine Bubble

Throughout 1928 Darling continued his series of cartoons drawing attention to the overvalued market. This cartoon appeared on November 15, 1928. Less than a year later the market crashed and financial panic ensued.

Being a Jack the Giant Killer Ain't What It Used to Be

When the Federal Reserve did move to curb stock market speculation in 1929, businesses and the economy suffered.

The End of the Bear Hunt

At the end of his series of cartoons of 1928 and 1929 that warned of the consequences of speculating in an overheated market, Ding drew the final chapter. This cartoon appeared on October 26, 1929.

The Toughest Dictator of Them All

Beginning in the early 1930s, the leading economists in the country's colleges and universities lectured that the national debt "does not make any difference because we owe it to ourselves." They continued to teach that theory until late in the twentieth century. In this 1940 cartoon, however, Darling used his common sense to disagree.

Easier to Get In Than to Get Out

As governments, businesses, and individuals have all discovered, it is far easier to fall into the debt trap than to get out. Ding drew this cartoon in 1938 as government deficits skyrocketed.

The Ravages of Peace

In 1940 Darling illustrated the impact of the New Deal on the U.S. Treasury.

Remodeling the U.S. Treasury to Suit the Tenant

When debt ceilings were reached, Congress remodeled the ceiling.

You Can Start a Fire with Gasoline—
but It's Awfully Hard to Put Out

Ding had a healthy fear of inflation and frequently portrayed its dangers.

Said the Man to His Own Shadow

By 1944 wages and prices were spiraling up rapidly. In their negotiations, neither management nor labor admitted any relationship between the two forces.

Senator George on Taxation

Ding was adept at paraphrasing long speeches with a simple drawing and a very few words.

"Rubber Dollars" Might Be Bad Economics
But, Oh Boy, Would They Come In Handy Now

Darling preached the evils of currency debasement, but even he acknowledged the temptation in this 1932 Christmas cartoon, a self-portrait that included his young family.

Conservation

Although during his lifetime the general public knew Ding Darling as an editorial cartoonist, his most significant and lasting contributions were as a pioneering conservationist. As Chairman of the Iowa State Conservation Commission in the early 1930s, he succeeded in revamping the constitution of that group. No longer were the Commissioners chosen on the basis of their hunting and fishing trips with the Governor, but upon professional qualification. During his tenure, Ding devised a Twenty-Five-Year Conservation Plan that still serves as model for management of natural resources in Iowa and in other states. Realizing that a good plan had to have a reference point, Darling hired Aldo Leopold to conduct the first inventory of Iowa's natural resources.

After serving so ably in Iowa, Ding was invited to Washington to become the Chief of the U.S. Biological Survey, the forerunner of the U.S. Fish & Wildlife Service. There he revitalized a moribund agency and guided the Federal Duck Stamp Act through Congress. Under the Duck Stamp Act waterfowl hunters must purchase a stamp to affix to their hunting licenses. All revenues from stamp sales are used to purchase and protect wildlife habitat in National Wildlife Refuges across the country. Since its inception the Federal Duck Stamp Program has enabled the purchase of more than five million acres of habitat. Through their purchases of Duck Stamps, hunters have in effect become stewards of wildlife.

Also during the 1930s, Darling instituted a federal, state, and private partnership called the Cooperative Fish & Wildlife Research Unit Program. As devised by Darling, the Research Unit Program would develop the basic information needed to make wise conservation decisions while at the same time providing an education for young men and women in academic disciplines that are potentially supportive to conservation management. Although the program is little known outside of conservation circles, it has grown from the first unit at Iowa State College (now Iowa State University) to more than fifty units across the country today. It continues to provide the basic research critical to good management of the country's natural resources.

Having learned from experience that partnerships were the most effective tools to accomplish many of his goals, Darling took the lead in founding the National Wildlife Federation in 1934 and served as its first President. The Federation brought many diverse local conservation groups into one effective national organization that would have a significant impact in Washington. As Darling pointed out, "Wildlife does not have a vote, so it is up to us to speak for them." The National Wildlife Federation today has several million members, and it continues to speak for wildlife and natural resources.

Despite so many enduring contributions, one could plausibly argue that Ding Darling's greatest impact was as an educator. Long before words like "ecology" were in fashion, when citizens felt that natural resources were unlimited and the unhindered use of those resources was a God-given right, Ding wrote that careful use of the country's resources was necessary to the future health and wealth of the nation. Throughout his long career, he peppered the public with conservation cartoons that drew the public's attention to the pragmatic need for wise resource use.

Wonder What Mother Will Say
When She Finds He's Had It Clipped

Ding Darling was among the first to recognize the need to conserve the nation's natural resources. Unbridled clear-cutting without replanting was standard forestry procedure when Ding drew this 1921 cartoon. It exemplified Darling's style: an important message combined with sufficient humor to catch the reader's attention.

What Does Mere Man
Know about the Perils of Non-Stop Flight?

Ding recognized that migratory birds need resting places along the nation's flyways in order to survive. During his tenure as Chief of the U.S. Biological Survey, he laid the practical foundation for building a coherent system of National Wildlife Refuges. Today that system incorporates more than 500 National Wildlife Refuges, many of which lie along major migratory routes.

When Prodigal Son Meets Prodigal Father

Darling believed that the future of the nation depended upon the wise use of its natural resources. That concept is becoming more self-evident now, but when Ding drew this cartoon in 1936, it was not. In speeches across the country in the 1930s, Darling pointed out that the great civilizations of history all disappeared when they depleted their natural resources.

How Rich Will We Be
When We Have Converted All Our Forests, All Our Soil,
All Our Water Resources and Minerals into Cash?

This question "How Rich Will We Be . . ." seemed heretical when Ding asked it in 1938. Today we recognize the wisdom of the question and the answer brings a shudder.

What Man Does to the Most Beautiful Gift of Nature—the River

Rivers the world over were once thought to be a natural dumping ground. Still today, there are individuals and companies that view rivers as the most cost-efficient means for disposing of their waste. Ding drew this cartoon in 1923.

Time to Take an Inventory of Our Pantry

Drawing this cartoon in 1936, when our abundant natural resources were being taken for granted, Ding reached a diverse national audience. A common theme throughout his cartoons, speeches, and articles was the need for wise stewardship, driving home the point that squandering resources leads to poverty and widespread war.

Providing for the Future

Darling was a man who looked to the future. Only if natural resources were managed wisely, he felt, would the next generations have a future. He drew this cartoon in 1926.

The Charge of the Nature Lovers Brigade

Being a nature lover does not necessarily make one a conservationist. Darling drew several other cartoons with the same theme as this 1929 cartoon, among them "Look Out, Here Come the Nature Lovers" and "We Do Hope the Wildflowers Appreciate How Much We Love Them."

Why We Go to Europe for Beautiful Scenery

By 1930 outdoor advertising was taking its toll on highway beauty.

- 1920 -

1930

- 1940 -

What a Few More Seasons Will Do to the Ducks

In 1930 disappearing habitat, drought, and over-hunting had reduced waterfowl populations to alarming levels. Darling believed that the disappearance of any species boded poorly for mankind. "As go ducks, so goes man."

48

Nobody's Constituents

By the end of his assignment as Chief of the U.S. Biological Survey, Darling had formed a good idea of why wildlife was suffering at the hands of politicians: wildlife had no votes to cast. He drew this cartoon in 1936, soon after leaving office.

The Conservation Interests Can Get What They Need If They Pull Together

Since wildlife did not have a vote, Darling figured that it was up to the nation's sportsmen to represent them. Although hunting and even fishing are now politically incorrect in some circles, it is a fact that the hunters and fishermen of America were its first effective conservationists.

IT'S HARD TO START A FIRE WITH ONE STICK OF WOOD

BUT IF YOU COULD GET THE FIREWOOD TOGETHER IN ONE PILE...

Darling believed that the many different conservation organizations that had started in the 1930s were politically ineffective. Vowing to give them clout, he founded the National Wildlife Federation and served as its first President. The National Wildlife Federation now has millions of sportsmen and sportswomen members who speak forcefully for wildlife.

Don't Say It—Sign It!

Having been a professional political observer for decades, Darling had become leery of political promises. Here his advice to conservationists was "get it in writing."

The History of Utopia

Ding drew this cartoon, also titled "The Outline of History," in 1936. It has been widely reprinted and copied, frequently without attribution. Rather than take offense at this plagiarism, Darling was delighted to have his message repeated.

What That Mud in Our Rivers Adds Up to Each Year

As a resident of an agricultural state, Darling was very concerned with soil erosion. Ding suggested that "the top soil which goes swirling by in our rivers at flood stage may look like mud to you but it is beefsteak and potatoes, ham and eggs and homemade bread with jam on it." On his own farm, which was not subject to water erosion, he planted tree lines in the 1930s to reduce the effects of wind erosion.

The Only Kettle She's Got

Although in his earlier years Darling had concentrated on specific conservation needs, by the end of his career he had come to believe that the greatest threat to the preservation of our planet was mankind's geometric growth in population.

The Race with the Stork

Darling's lifetime saw the progression from horse and buggy travel to air travel, a transition he neatly adapted to Malthusian theory. Since he drew this cartoon a half-century ago, events have clearly demonstrated that food production cannot keep up with the geometric progression of the world's expanding population.

As Land Goes, So Goes Man

Ding Darling lived on the unspoiled prairie in the late 1800s. He had seen the land converted to agriculture, and the result of unwise agricultural practices.

[Untitled]

When Darling served as Chief of the U.S. Biological Survey, he instituted many programs to enhance wildlife. Those programs are still viable today and have proved that wise management of natural resources leads to the recovery of endangered species.

WHAT WE HAVE DONE TO THE NATURAL BEAUTIES OF OUR LANDSCAPE.

WHAT NATURE WILL DO TO RESTORE IT IF GIVEN A CHANCE.

[Untitled]

Despite the bad conservation news of recent years, the good news is that nature will indeed restore itself when given the opportunity.

Problems New and Old

Most of us tend to think of today's problems as unique to our current generation. Ding Darling's cartoons prove otherwise.

A Little Louder, No One Seems to Hear You

While most of us are convinced that we live in a particularly violent era, Darling's Ordinary Citizen felt the same way in 1925.

After All the Trouble We Had Catching Them

If you guessed this cartoon was drawn yesterday, you missed by the better part of a century. Darling drew this cartoon dealing with crowded prisons and release of un-rehabilitated criminals in 1927, more than seventy-five years ago.

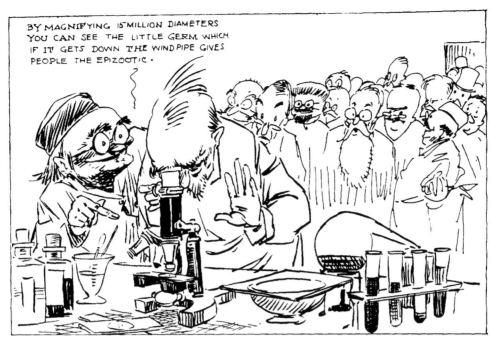

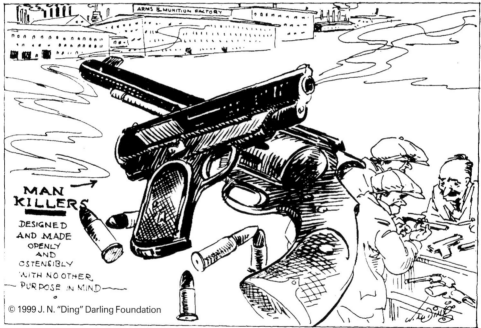

Straining at a Gnat and Swallowing a Camel

Most people, especially young people, tend to think of today's problems as unique to our own particular point in time. The proliferation of guns and violence, they assume, is a product of today's society. Darling, however, was dealing with the need for gun control in 1924, long before most of us were born.

As a hunter, Ding distinguished long guns (shotguns and rifles) from handguns, which he felt had no other purpose than to kill human beings.

If A Banker Did It, We'd Send Him Up for Life

With few exceptions since Ding drew this cartoon in 1938, the Social Security Trust Fund has been used by Congress to artificially "reduce" government deficits. On those rare occasions that a surplus has been forecast, there has been little interest in repaying the borrowed monies.

The Ascent of Man—Final Stage

Ding drew this cartoon in 1941, noting that science and invention seem often to cause more problems than they cure.

The Atom Is on the Loose

Immediately following the dropping of the atomic bomb, Ding drew this cartoon. Far from whimsical, the cartoon foresaw the problems that would face the world in the years to come.

Tired of Giving? You Don't Know What It Is to Be Tired

Ding drew this cartoon in 1917 during the First World War. He hoped that civilization would never again witness the plight of refugees displaced by wars of aggression. Unfortunately, the image was just as poignant when it was reprinted during the Second World War, and it remains relevant today.

Bigots and Such

Jay Darling lived in an age when social stigma based on race and religion was widely accepted as a fact of life. Despite the fact that he was a white, wealthy Protestant, his personal sense of humanity led him to rebel against society's "norm." It is a credit to Darling's ethics that he criticized society's accepted prejudices, and it is a credit to his cartooning skills that he conveyed his sense of humanity so effectively.

The Burden Which the White Man Laid Down

When Darling drew this cartoon in 1915, most Americans thought that the end of slavery marked the end of their obligation to citizens of African-American descent. "Ding" recognized that despite their newly legislated status, black people did not yet have equal opportunities. He urged progress in social status as well as legal status.

And We Have Been Finding Fault with Mexico

In 1919, Darling found equal fault with both white bigots and black bigots as they vented their prejudices. The disappointment and disgust of the general public is reflected in Uncle Sam's face.

A Good Motto but Why the Disguise?

Fresh from victory in the First World War, the United States was flushed with patriotic pride in "Americanism." Unfortunately, the term was soon adopted by racial bigots as the dubious rationale to justify their bigotry.

Making the Citizens Over into 100% Americans?

By 1923, the general public had become intimidated by bigotry. Racial zealots continued to use the term "Americanism" to justify their prejudices, just as they do today.

When a Local Mandate Becomes Everybody's Business

Arabs vs. Jews, Protestants vs. Catholics, Whites vs. Blacks, Serbs vs. Albanians: there seems no end to the opportunity for racial and religious strife, and as Darling pointed out, too few voices willing to remind us of our common humanity.

Even the Best Flag in the World Has Its Shadow

In cartoons throughout his career, "Ding" expressed his deep conviction that the United States is the land of opportunity, the land of freedom and justice for all. At the same time he painfully and publicly recognized that his country had serious flaws. He eloquently expressed these two divergent emotions in this 1939 cartoon.

The Ordinary Citizen

Ninety years ago Ding Darling dedicated the first anthology of his cartoons to the "Ordinary Citizen." The long-suffering Ordinary Citizen appeared in many roles in Darling's cartoons, sometimes as a consumer, sometimes as a voter, and sometimes as an aggrieved spouse. Most frequently, however, Ding's long-suffering Ordinary Citizen was the taxpayer.

As will be seen in the following pages, Darling did not always sympathize with the ordinary citizen; sometimes he was soundly critical.

The role of the Ordinary Citizen has not changed much in the past century. He or she remains easily recognized.

They Don't Even Slow Down

This cartoon was first published at tax time in 1932. It was reprinted in 1949. The puzzle remains: "Find the man who pays for the car."

The Game Is Getting Decidedly Monotonous

In 1927 the ball seemed to get past the legal system all too frequently.

The Blinded Samson

As work stoppages crippled more industries in 1919, Darling used the Ordinary Citizen to appeal for more restraint in the exercise of labor's right to strike.

We're Not So Much Interested in Who Has the Right of Way as Where Is a Safety Zone

As the strength of the labor movement increased in the 1920s, the frequent clashes between Labor and Management often worked to the disadvantage of the Ordinary Citizen.

Quite a Family to Be Responsible For

Throughout his long career, which lasted more than a half-century, Darling scolded the public for its indifference and apathy toward government. Here, in 1929, the Ordinary Citizen contemplates the product of that indifference.

Fighting King George for the Right to Our Own Judges
and Courts in 1776—and Resigning in Favor of King
Kleagle of the Invisible Empire in 1923

Always disgusted by the apathy of the general public, Darling castigated his "Ordinary Citizen" for his lack of resolve in dealing with organized bigotry.

The Extreme Perversity of Nature

As an avid gardener and member of several Garden Clubs, Ding used the Ordinary Citizen to empathize with gardeners the world over.

Wanted: More and Better Scientists

The Ordinary Citizen was frequently caught between extremes. In December 1930, Darling portrayed him torn between the extreme expansion of the late 1920s and the extraordinary collapse that followed.

Not as Nature Intended

Ding recognized that it was not only at tax time that the Ordinary Citizen suffered. Have you recently stood in line at the Drivers License Bureau or, for that matter, any other bureau of government?

Father Helps with the Christmas Decorations

Although Darling was a skilled artist and quite good with his hands, we can easily imagine where he got the inspiration for this 1937 portrait of the Ordinary Citizen.

We Pump Enough to Drown All of 'Em,
If It Wasn't for the Leaks

Darling drew this cartoon in 1916, relatively early in his career. Although his drawing skills were not fully developed, his ability to illustrate an idea was clearly mature. So, too, was his empathy for the Ordinary Citizen and taxpayer.

91

Revising Our Tax Schedule

Although the federal budget in 1921 was less than 1% of its present figure, it still weighed heavily on the Ordinary Citizen, and Congress's solution was much the same as it is today.

The Incorrigible Flirt

In 1924 the Ordinary Citizen—shown here as the taxpayer, labor, farmer, and business—bore the weight of Congressional spending.

Picture of a Gentleman Helping His Wife Pick Out Wallpaper

Darling drew this cartoon of the Ordinary Citizen helping his wife pick out wallpaper in 1916. Many stores still have those little chairs where the dutiful spouse may sit quietly while such weighty decisions are made.

94

Holidays and Other Special Days

In this day and age, when many people are unsure about the significance of Memorial Day or even the Fourth of July, it helps to be reminded why they are special days. Ding Darling never let a holiday pass without reminding his readers of the reason for that holiday. Similarly, he always noted other special days, such as the first day of school or the official arrival of Spring.

A Nice, New, Clean Page

Darling noted the beginning of every New Year, often reflecting the highlights of the past year and commenting on prospects for the coming one. In this New Year's cartoon, he reflects on human nature and learning (see dialogue in background).

There Was a Day When the Responsibilities of Government
Were Taken Seriously

Although Presidents' Day was not celebrated in Darling's time as such, he always took advantage of the approach of Lincoln's and Washington's birthdays to remind politicians of their best heritage.

Love's Labor Lost

Usually an optimist, Darling expressed his dismay on Valentine's Day, 1927, at the marked increase in divorces.

Early Training Will Tell

Ding did not often note religious holidays, but on occasion he did use the opportunity for humor. Here he takes a poke at both his own golf game and child psychology.

Wait Until Mother Takes Up the Forty-Hour Week

Ding drew this cartoon in 1936 as a commentary on the New Deal proposal to reduce the work week to forty hours. The cartoon has been widely reprinted on Mother's Day, and it is reprinted here with the acknowledgment that there is no occupation more demanding of skill, patience, intelligence, strength, and stamina than Motherhood.

What Did St. George Know about Dragons, Anyway?

Perhaps because he was not a very good student himself, Darling remembered years later the sinking feeling that final exams produce. He never forgot that between "The Enchanted Valley of Summer" and himself lay final examinations.

Lest We Who Inherit Its Blessings Forget
Who Gave and Preserved for Us This Nation

Whether in the image drawn or the title conceived, Darling took pains to ensure each Memorial Day cartoon carried a heartfelt acknowledgement of the sacrifices made by earlier generations.

© 1999 J.N. "Ding" Darling Foundation

Freedom Has Never Called to Us in Vain

This 1918 Flag Day cartoon was also published under the title "Never for Conquest, Ever for Freedom." Scholars researching Darling's cartoons are frustrated when they learn that Darling sometimes published the same cartoon under different titles and sometimes used the same title for different cartoons.

Buying Our Human Rights in 1776—
and Selling Them to the New Deal Politicians in 1936

Darling used the occasion of Independence Day, 1936, to express his concern about New Deal spending. Although he had been supportive of government programs to stimulate the nation's economy in the early thirties, by 1936 he became alarmed that the politicians had discovered that they could buy the citizens' votes with the citizens' money. It is a lesson that politicians have never forgotten.

That Sad Moment When Father Realizes He's a Has-Been

Darling's insights into human nature produced many a chuckle of recognition.
This 1928 cartoon is dedicated to aging fathers and grandfathers the world over.

A Nice, Quiet Fourth

Darling addressed the nation's complacency in this prophetic cartoon of July 4, 1941.
By year's end the United States was enmeshed in World War II.

107

Labor Day

When Darling drew this Labor Day cartoon in 1926, the average worker put in ten hours of labor each day, six days a week. A real holiday was perhaps even more welcome then than it is now.

Vacation's Over

No matter how long it's been since one had to go back to school in the fall, this feeling is well remembered.

If We're Not Thankful, We Ought to Be

Darling drew this cartoon in 1940. He ranked Thanksgiving among the nation's most important holidays.

Here's Wishing Everybody a Happy New Year

As one of the worst years in America's financial history passed, Darling did his best to convey optimism for the next year, 1931.

Presidents

Darling drew through the terms of eight different Presidents. Although he tailored his cartoons to the personality, character, and legislative goals of each individual President, he took a common approach to all. First, he gave each man a fair start. Second, he attempted to draw cartoons showing both sides of any significant debate. Finally, when any President died, whether in office or later, Darling attempted to pay tribute to the man's best qualities.

The Next Great War

In 1915 Darling drew this cartoon reflecting the great debate between President Woodrow Wilson and former President Theodore Roosevelt, a difference aptly described by the slogans on the placards with which they are attempting to beat each other.

The Long, Long Trail

When Theodore Roosevelt (1858–1919) died, Darling drew this fitting tribute to one of his favorite Presidents. The image was widely reprinted, becoming perhaps the most widely published cartoon of its time. Reproductions of the cartoon in other media, such as bronze, appear in many of the schools across the nation that are named for this popular President.

Uncle Bill Taft Seems to Think
That Swing Was Built to Swing In

Like others, Ding was not particularly fond of William Howard Taft (1857–1930), and he appears in few of Darling's cartoons. One suspects, however, that the cartoonist was grateful that Taft's obese physique and tonsorial qualities lent themselves to easy caricature. Darling also appreciated Taft's support for the League of Nations, which both men strongly favored.

A Perfectly Hopeless Undertaking

Woodrow Wilson (1856–1924) appeared in at least 225 Darling cartoons during his Presidency, 1913–21. Although Wilson was a Democrat and Darling was a staunch Republican, the majority of those cartoons are pro-Wilson.

Will It Bring Back an Olive Branch or a Mailed Gauntlet?

Ding drew Wilson's unending peace efforts in the most favorable light and admired his courageous persistence despite criticism from both within and without the Democratic Party.

A Ticklish Moment

Textbooks following Wilson's Presidency from 1913 to 1921 have tended to paint him as a naïve Pacifist. This Darling cartoon and others like it, however, indicate that Wilson clearly desired to negotiate from a position of armed strength.

120

Let's Take a Lesson from History

When Woodrow Wilson was subjected to the most severe criticism, Darling drew this 1918 cartoon likening his stoic persistence to that of a previous President.

The Art Student's Masterpiece and the
Professor's Criticism

Whenever Wilson made progress toward a peace treaty, the Senate—led by such notables as Henry Cabot Lodge—quickly showed him the error of his ways.

The Peace Which in Life Was Denied Him

Ding drew this moving cartoon when Woodrow Wilson died in 1924. It alludes, of course, to the peace efforts which had occupied most of Wilson's Presidency.

And No Shepherd Has Since Come Forth to Take His Place

Not entirely satisfied with the eulogy that he had drawn two days earlier, Darling
drew this tribute to Wilson's leadership on February 6, 1924.

There's a Gentleman Waiting to Be Introduced

When Warren Gamaliel Harding ran for President in 1920, few had ever heard of him. Ding used his Ordinary Citizen to portray the public's need to know more about the candidate.

We Doubt If the Best Mother-in-Law in the World Would Be Much of an Asset Along on the Honeymoon

Whereas Ding Darling was more than willing to allow each new President the traditional "honeymoon" free from negative comment, the U.S. Senate was not.

The Same Corner Where We Ran Off the Track Last Trip

Soon after he took office, it became apparent that President Harding was going to face the same obstacle to reaching a disarmament and peace accord as had his predecessors.

There's Plenty More [Big] Game in the Woods for Those Who Know How to Shoot

When Harding made significant progress during the first year of his Presidency, Darling showed Congress as anxious to take the credit.

AN ORPHAN AT 8 IS NOW ONE OF THE WORLD'S GREATEST MINING ENGINEERS AND ECONOMISTS WHOSE AMBITION IS TO ELIMINATE THE CYCLE OF DEPRESSION AND UNEMPLOYMENT

THE SON OF A PLASTERER IS NOW THE WORLD'S GREATEST NEUROLOGIST AND HIS HOBBY IS GOOD HEALTH FOR POOR CHILDREN

A PRINTER'S APPRENTICE IS NOW CHIEF EXECUTIVE OF THE UNITED STATES

DRAWN IN 1923 BY J.N. DARLING AND AWARDED THE PULITZER PRIZE FOR THE BEST U.S. CARTOON OF THE YEAR —

BUT THEY DIDN'T GET THERE BY HANGING AROUND THE CORNER DRUG STORE

In Good Old U.S.A.

Darling won his first Pulitzer Prize for this cartoon, drawn in 1923. Warren G. Harding was the Chief Executive referred to in panel three. Herbert Hoover was the mining engineer referred to in panel one, and Dr. Frederick Peterson was the Mayo Clinic neurologist in panel two. Darling believed that anyone who was hardworking and diligent in the pursuit of his goals would achieve them.

Harding Is Dead

When Harding died in office, Darling drew a bereaved Uncle Sam.

Goodbye and Good Luck

When Calvin Coolidge (1872–1933) became President in 1923, replacing Warren Harding, Darling drew this somber cartoon.

Atta Boy, Cal, If You Want It Done Well
Do It Yourself

Soon after Coolidge took office, he was faced with the Harding administration's Teapot Dome scandal. He immediately began a thorough cleaning of the Republican Party.

Begins to Look As If We Never Would
Get Out of This Jerkwater Town

Like Warren Harding and Woodrow Wilson before him, Calvin Coolidge was an internationalist. Unfortunately he faced the same recalcitrant U.S. Senate, which continued in its obstructionist role.

The Daily Grind in Washington

Although "Cal" Coolidge was mild in his demeanor, Darling pictured him taking a more aggressive attitude toward Congress than had his predecessors.

Might As Well Be Going

When all efforts to entice Calvin Coolidge to run again for President failed, Ding captured the feeling of the forlorn Republican Party.

So Long and Good Luck

Ding had admired Calvin Coolidge as a man and as a President. When Coolidge did retire from office, Darling drew an appreciative Uncle Sam.

AN ORPHAN AT 10

HOOVER

PRESIDENT OF THE UNITED STATES AT 54

While Such Things Are Possible
There Is Nothing Wrong with Our Country

When Herbert Clark Hoover (1874–1964) took office, Ding welcomed him with this cartoon. Ding, who also came from modest beginnings, openly admired Hoover and his many accomplishments. They became personal friends and remained so for the remainder of their lives.

The Difference

While Hoover campaigned for the Presidency 1928, Darling drew this graphic capturing the difference between the two candidates' credentials. Hoover had an extraordinary record of previous public service, both at home and abroad.

Gulliver and the Lilliputians

Like his predecessors, Hoover faced a recalcitrant Congress. Darling held Congress, here likened unto the Lilliputians, responsible for Hoover's failure to achieve his progressive goals.

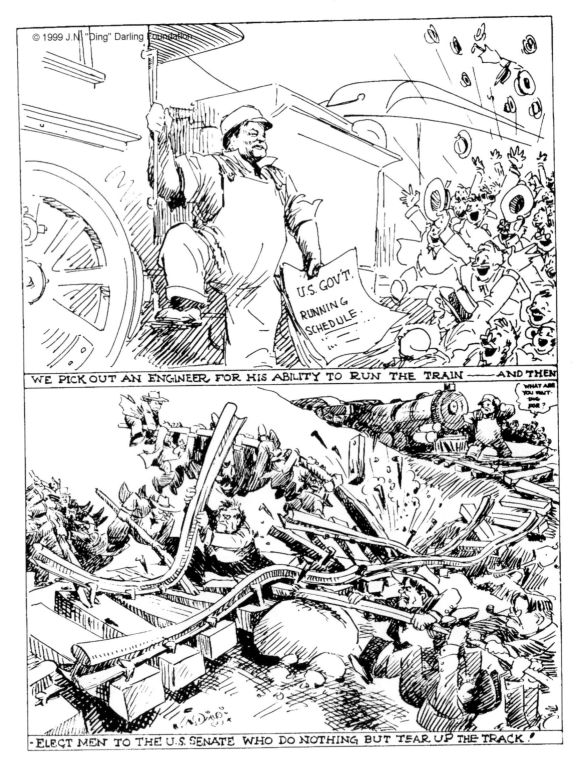

WE PICK OUT AN ENGINEER FOR HIS ABILITY TO RUN THE TRAIN —— AND THEN

- ELECT MEN TO THE U.S. SENATE WHO DO NOTHING BUT TEAR UP THE TRACK !

Aren't We Odd?

After the Crash of 1929, Darling again portrayed the U.S. Senate as the reason for Hoover's failure to respond with successful legislation. Some of the Senate's most habitual naysayers are pictured tearing up the track.

A Good Republican

When Hoover, a Republican, was defeated in 1932 by Democrat Franklin Delano Roosevelt (1882–1945), Darling paid this last tribute to Hoover's sense of duty and responsibility.

No Back Seat Driving

During Roosevelt's unprecedented four terms in office, Darling drew an equally unprecedented 400 cartoons in which Roosevelt was a central figure. Initially, during Roosevelt's first term, Darling's cartoons were quite supportive. In this 1933 drawing, the Ordinary Citizen admires Roosevelt's handling of Congress.

Starting the Works

Roosevelt's mastery of Congress enabled him to begin a massive public works
program to combat the unemployment of the early 1930s.

143

And So After All These Years!

Ding even went so far as to paint Roosevelt as the hero rescuing the fair damsel.

Once to Every Man and Nation Comes a Moment to Decide

Although Ding was a Republican, he was frequently as critical of management as he was of labor leadership. Despite the fact that he would have been horrified at the actual nationalization of industry, he admired Roosevelt's use of that threat to encourage businesses to police their own practices.

Political? No, Certainly Not

By the time Roosevelt's first term was ending, Darling had become alarmed at the administration's unabashed use of government spending to buy political favor. Although such political spending was not new, the amounts available under New Deal budgets for these purposes were unprecedented and staggering.

But Captain! He Might Need It Sometime Himself

When the Supreme Court hampered Roosevelt in pursuing his goals, he went after the Court with a vengeance. Darling likened Roosevelt's action to attempting to take Uncle Sam's life vest.

Dollars to Doughnuts They Don't Both Make the Curve

As New Deal spending continued, Darling showed the basic conflict between Roosevelt's promises.

Taking His Girlfriend for a Ride

By the middle of the President's second term, Ding showed him in full control of the Democratic Party.

Blaming It on the Roof

In 1939, when the spending policies of the New Deal threatened to exceed regulatory limits on the national debt, Roosevelt argued that the debt was not too great, the ceiling was too low. That logic has been presented by many administrations that followed, both Democratic and Republican.

Such Remarkable Talent

Putting a "positive spin" on troubling problems is not an invention of the current generation. This cartoon was drawn in 1939.

Junior's Piggy Bank

Alarmed at New Deal spending, Ding portrayed Roosevelt and Congress conspiring to deprive future generations.

Just a Lot of Nobodies Who Never Knew Nothin'

When Roosevelt ran for an unprecedented third term in office, Darling showed his predecessors and Uncle Sam as both disappointed and disapproving.

The Salve That Soothes but Never Heals

Franklin Roosevelt had a great gift for oratory, a gift that Ding Darling found less than satisfying.

The Direct Primary

This was one of the last Roosevelt cartoons that Darling drew. When Roosevelt decided to run for a fourth term, Darling pointed out that after three terms of growth under Roosevelt, the federal government and its employees had become a constituency in itself.

155

The Political Education of a Vice-Presidential Candidate

When President Roosevelt chose Harry S. Truman as his vice-presidential running mate in the 1944 elections, Darling found Truman's political heritage quite suspect. Although he was later exonerated of any personal wrongdoing, Truman had been closely associated with the Kansas City Pendergast Machine.

The Passengers Are Beginning to Sit Back and Relax

When Roosevelt died in office in 1945, Harry S. Truman (1884–1972) became President after serving less than three months as Vice-President. Truman was little known outside of his own state of Missouri and the U. S. Senate, where he had served as Senator. Taking office at a critical point in World War II, he was greeted by a nervous, skeptical public. Less than two months into his Presidency, Truman had proven his leadership and his decision-making abilities.

The Same Old Game but Bigger Chips

Many pundits doubted Truman's ability to negotiate effectively with seasoned leaders such as Churchill and Stalin, but Darling painted him as fully qualified. Truman was, in fact, a serious student of history and government.

How to Win Friends and Influence People

Ding greatly admired Truman's courage in dealing with the railroad unions.
Although Truman was closely associated with the labor movement, he
demonstrated that he would put the nation's economic well-being ahead of
that of the railroad unions. Willing to invoke the wrath and indignation of the
union, he placed their significant campaign funding in jeopardy.

Oh Look What Harry Truman Found in the White House Attic

Throughout his Presidency, Truman was straightforward and brutally honest. Darling greatly admired those two qualities, which he felt had become increasingly rare in public figures.

How Very Old-Fashioned!

Unlike so many politicians before him and after him, Truman refused to invoke class differences for political advantage. Darling pictured an Uncle Sam delighted by Truman's personal integrity.

Speak to Him Right Sharply, Harry

Truman faced strong inflationary pressures during his Presidency. Here Darling pictures him pleading with the inflationary genie as two labor leaders and a business leader pump merrily away, further inflating the genie.

The End of the Ninth Inning

When Harry S. Truman ran for President in 1948, all the public opinion polls and political pundits said that he would be defeated by his opponent, Thomas Dewey, in a humiliating landslide. Nonetheless, as shown here by Darling in a cartoon published a few days before the election, Truman continued to campaign gamely.

Who Killed Cock Robin?

Despite the polls and the pundits, Truman handily defeated Dewey in the 1948 Presidential election. Later the pundits argued loudly about what factors had led to Truman's victory. Here, a few days later, Darling attributed the victory to Truman himself, strongly backed by organized labor.

Politics and Politicians

Editorial cartoonists are frequently considered political cartoonists. In Darling's case nearly one-third of his cartoons are indexed under the subject "politics." As can be seen, politics and politicians have not changed much over time.

Good Heavens, Maybe We've Been Doing It Wrong

Ding noted that there was not necessarily a correlation between performance in a campaign and performance in office.

The Governing Class

Ding pulled no punches when he expressed his disappointment in public apathy.

The New National and International Champion

Ding Darling came from the age when "a man's word was his bond."

You Gotta Be a Liberal to Get Votes These Days

Darling had supported the New Deal when fiscal stimulus was obviously needed, but by 1936 he felt that the need for such magnanimous spending had passed.

What's In a Name?

The political concept of misleading the public with an artful choice of words is not new. When a proposal to change the name of the Department of the Interior to the Department of Conservation surfaced in 1936, Ding drew this lampoon.

Now—All Together

No matter which party is in control of Congress, it always seems inclined toward wasteful spending. Ding drew this cartoon in 1916, nearly a century ago.

Maybe If They'd Try Scalding
They Could Get a Few More Pin Feathers

If Darling's 1916 caricature of Congress behaving as a pig at the trough was too strong, this 1923 cartoon carried the same message with more humor.

Speaking of the Redistribution of Wealth!

Ding may have pained politicians with this 1936 cartoon, but it continues to strike most taxpayers as an accurate depiction.

Running Wide Open

Ding called the public's attention to federal spending for political purposes in 1930.

Another Fat One for the Pot

Darling suspected that, whatever else it might be, Social Security would be a plump target for political cannibalization, a suspicion that was well founded.

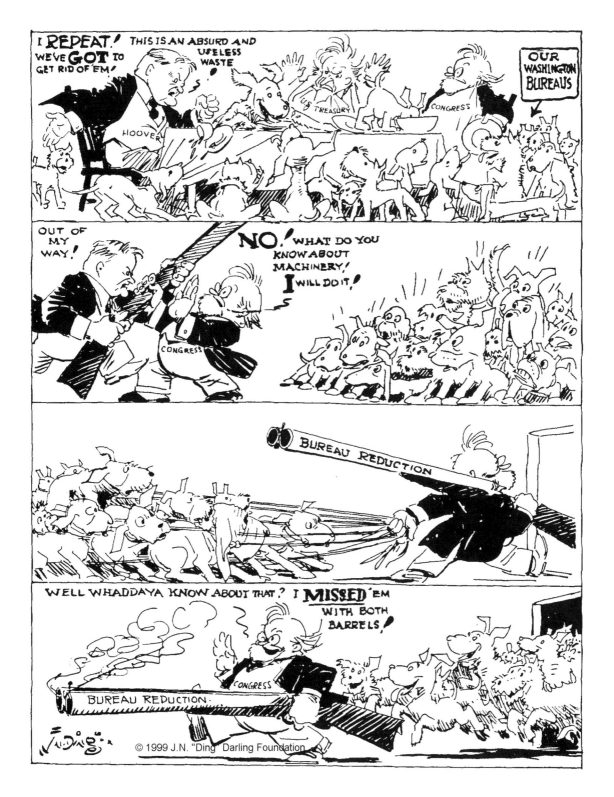

Getting Rid of Our National Pets

As Darling indicated in 1936, Congress always seems to fall short in its promise to reduce bureaucracy.

Your Obedient Servant

Congress can be dangerous with an axe in hand.

Maybe We Should Take a General Anesthetic

Darling was sufficiently realistic to know that despite the public's desire for a reduction in government spending, they were always the first to complain when their own favorite programs were reduced.

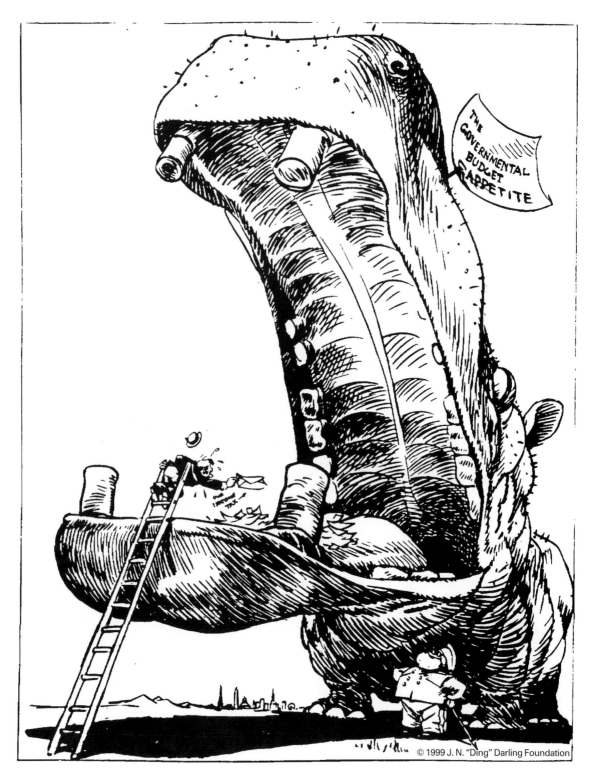

Well, Here Goes!

Little seems to have changed since Darling drew this 1923 impression of how the taxpayer views government operations.

Now She'll Never Go Home!

Briefly in 1926, there was a significant budget surplus. There were many who wanted to help spend that surplus.

They Always Look Good in Their Own Training Quarters

No matter whether one attends the Democratic or the Republican National Convention, he or she becomes convinced that the other party doesn't stand a chance in the upcoming elections.

The Biennial Tug of War Is Now On

It's always a struggle to get the incumbents out of power.

Now All We Have To Do Is Clean Up the Dirt

Following each campaign, there seems to be mud left on the Capitol's steps.

The Presidency of the United States

Ding drew this cartoon near the end of his friend President Herbert Hoover's term. Perhaps Darling foresaw a time when vilification would discourage qualified individuals from running for political office.

War and Peace

Jay Darling drew through two World Wars and numerous lesser conflicts. He was attuned to the suffering caused by war, and his cartoons conveyed to noncombatants that suffering. He portrayed the efforts to end those wars and to avoid future wars. He was a fervent supporter of the League of Nations, and he was indignant when the U.S. Senate, jealously guarding its prerogative over foreign treaties, undermined all efforts to create an international peace organization.

As an ardent conservationist, he urged the wise use of the world's natural resources, arguing that history demonstrated when a nation's population outstripped its natural resources, conflict with neighbors inevitably followed.

Although Ding was more than willing to fight when necessary, he judged all wars as failures of mankind's ability to reason.

We Have Gained 200 Yards of the Enemy Trenches
Dispatch from the Front—1916

Darling was adept at personalizing impersonal messages, as in this 1916 cartoon from World War I.

Sign Him Up Before He Gets Over His Headache

Ding believed the most opportune time to create a world peace organization was immediately following a war, before the pubic forgot its horrors. This cartoon was drawn in support of the League of Nations, following World War I.

The Round Trip to the Disarmament Conference

While this cartoon may appear light-hearted, Darling was dismayed that all efforts to create a world peace organization were failures.

Isn't It About Time We Decided on a Remedy and Took Some?

In the lull between two World Wars, Darling expressed his disappointment that the League of Nations had failed to materialize.

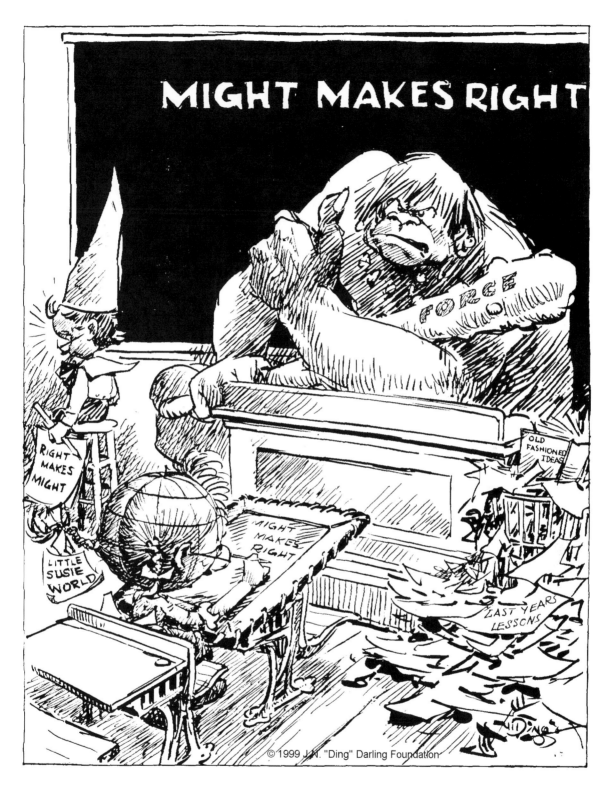

All Our Lessons to Do Over Again

In 1938, as Hitler invaded his neighbors in the prelude to World War II, Ding drew this cartoon.

Bluebeard's Seventh Wife

Between each German invasion of its neighbors, Hitler talked peace. Darling viewed those peace overtures with the same skepticism as this prospective bride.

The Progress of Civilization

When Ding was especially disappointed with the human race, he frequently pointed out that not much seems to have been learned in the evolutionary process.

The Voice of Experience

Only two months before the United States became embroiled in World War II, Darling portrayed an apathetic United States.

Waiting for the Sword to Fall

Darling continued to portray the horrors of war and aggression in this cartoon from
World War II.

A Tough Old Oak

Even before the entry of the United States into war as England's ally, Britain was deflecting Germany's superior military forces.

Remember!

This widely reprinted Darling cartoon appeared on the first anniversary of the Japanese sneak attack on Pearl Harbor, the event that immediately brought the United States into World War II.

The Sleeping Giant and the Lilliputian

Ding Darling and Japanese Admiral Yamamoto, the architect of the raid on Pearl Harbor, had one thing in common: they both believed that Japan had awakened a sleeping giant.

A Horse, a Horse, a Kingdom for a Horse

Adolf Hitler was not the first to find Russian winters inhospitable. Ding believed that those who ignored history were certain to repeat earlier mistakes.

201

As Inevitable as Time

Although Ding usually reserved such graphics to call attention to victims of aggression, in this case he shows Germany's military losses. Since the cartoon was drawn only shortly after the United States entered the war, it is possible that he intended it as encouragement to America and its allies.

Cutting Their Pudding Before It's Baked

Ding thought the Axis Powers were being a bit premature in
dividing up the free world.

Heil Hitler

By mid 1942 the German people had gone from the exhilaration of successful invasions to the sober realization that the Allies had far more resources available than did Germany.

Good News, Alas, Does Not Travel Alone!

During World War II, just as he had during World War I, Darling managed to convey the poignant suffering behind the headlines.

Eventually, Why Not Now?

Immediately following the dropping of the atom bomb in 1945, Ding Darling drew this cartoon. Although the cartoon drew little recognition, a few years after Darling's retirement, a nearly identical cartoon by another artist won the Pulitzer Prize. Darling's reaction was "plagiarism is the most sincere form of flattery."

Seed for the New Crop

As the end of World War II approached, Ding began urging the United States and its allies to think ahead.

And Brother, It's High Time

Darling was very concerned that efforts to found the United Nations might falter as had previous efforts to establish a League of Nations.

We Tried Everything but Dynamite

Following World War II, the world entered the Cold War. Darling pictured the unsuccessful efforts of the United Nations to lift the Iron Curtain.

The Final Verdict on Human Intelligence?

Largely because of the failure of the United States to participate, the League of Nations had proved ineffective, and Europe headed toward a war that would eventually involve the entire world. In this cartoon Darling obviously delivered his own verdict.

Epilogue

Jay Darling died in 1962 at the age of 86. In his life he drew more than 15,000 cartoons covering the gamut of human behavior. Although he doubted that any of his cartoons had ever changed the course of events, it is probable that his insights into the history, trends, thoughts, and politics of the United States served to inspire others.

The J. N. "Ding" Darling Foundation has collected more than 6,800 Darling cartoons and placed them on one CD-ROM. The collection is cross-indexed by date, title, subject, person, event, and key graphical element. It is unlikely that one can think of a subject or person from the first half of the twentieth century that is not covered in this collection. The CD is available for purchase by the public.

As Darling's health declined in his eighties, he drew a final farewell to his readers, which he gave to his secretary with instructions to print it after his death. The morning following his death, that cartoon was printed on the front page of the *Des Moines Register* exactly where his cartoons had appeared for the previous fifty years. It brought tears to the eyes of those many readers who had spent their entire lifetimes starting the day with a Ding cartoon.

Ding's Farewell

The Des Moines Register—Tuesday, Feb. 13, 1962